The Overlap of Things

To think that from this mean and broken bush
should come such joy ...
– Michael Walsh (1897–1938)

Margaret Nohilly

The Overlap of Things

ARLEN HOUSE

The Overlap of Things

is published in 2023 by

ARLEN HOUSE
42 Grange Abbey Road
Baldoyle
Dublin
D13 A0F3
Ireland
Email: arlenhouse@gmail.com
arlenhouse.ie

ISBN 978–1–85132–305–0, paperback

International distribution
SYRACUSE UNIVERSITY PRESS
621 Skytop Road, Suite 110
Syracuse
New York 13244–5290
USA
Email: supress@syr.edu
www.syracuseuniversitypress.syr.edu

Typesetting by Arlen House

Cover images:
'A Puddle of Leaves' and 'Maple Flame'
photography by the author

Contents

Acknowledgements

Thanks to the editors of the following publications where some of these poems first appeared: *Poetry Ireland Review; The Stony Thursday Book; Crannóg; Windows 20; Kindlings; Remembering Séan Cahill; The Longford Leader*, New Writing.

A version of 'Cornucopia' was runner-up in The Siarscéal Festival, Roscommon in 2012.

'La Sieste' was shortlisted in The Boyle Arts Festival in 2013.

'Finding Feet' was a response to artist Gerard Keaveney's 'Attachment' – collage & acrylic on board, as part of The Respond Project 2014 – an initiative of Longford County Arts Office in association with Backstage Theatre.

'Happenstance' was interpreted in a short film by Shelley Corcoran, *Leader* photographer, as part of Respond 2015.

'Joy of Books' was awarded 1st prize in the Inaugural Pádraic Colum Poetry Competition in 2018 - the poem was inspired by 'Picture Books in Winter' in Niall MacMonagle's 'What Lies Beneath' in the *Sunday Independent*.

'Bona Fide' was placed first in the Goldsmith Literary Festival Poetry Competition 2019, and both 'A Time for Everything' and 'October 2017' were shortlisted.

'Indomitable Wings' was a response to the RTÉ series *Ireland's Epic Women* in 2020.

'Promise' was read at 'Ireland Reads 2021' on Longford Library Facebook page; as were 'From Here to Where You Are' and 'Treasure Hunt' on Ireland Poetry Day 2021.

'Full Blown' was longlisted in St Francis Hospice Poetry 2022.

Sincere thanks to my poetry colleagues in Lanesboro and Longford, and to retired County Librarian, Mary Carleton Reynolds for unfailing support and encouragement; to the library staff, both past and present, and our new County Librarian, Martina Needham, for their gracious help and hospitality; to Jack Harte, Noel Monahan, the late Fergus Kennedy, County Arts Officer, Heather Brett, Eileen Sheehan, Paul Perry, Dennis Greig, John F. Deane, Grace Wells, who have influenced my writing in various ways; to my husband Tom and our family for constant inspiration and assistance, and especially to my sisters Dolores (my sounding block from start to finish), Miriam and Lucilla – ardent advocates, adept and generous critics.

Special thanks to Alan Hayes, Arlen House, for accepting my work and affording me this opportunity to share it.

for Dolores, Miriam, Lucilla
– and the late Michael

THE OVERLAP OF THINGS

Joy of Books
after Jessie Wilcox Smith

Just the little size of her,
not more than four or five –
scraggy, short brown hair,
mirth in her eyes;
ensconced in floral cushions
on a lattice window seat.

A glare from settled snow
illuminates the page she searches,
propped on drawn-up knees –
more books strewn round her feet –
oblivious to sounds within the house
or skirmishes outside.

How privileged this little girl
to be so captivated;
yet might not deprivation spark
a hunger for enlightenment,
escape, even a single book,
good-fortune-come-upon, could spur?

Though not a wide-eyed reader
as a child, I treasure books
as pearls, and poetry my element.
I pace my raid on novels: engagement
with new characters less riveting
than tinkering with words.

Letting Go

It took a while to find a safe place to veer off
the busy winding road to have my picnic lunch.

I'm not averse to taking tea in cafes, even on my own,
but this was novel, ritual, September stealth.

I chose my spot: an ample tarmac patch, car nook
unseen from someone's house. One o'clock: pupils,

teachers open books, obey the bell. I shrug and smile,
spread salad roll discreetly on my lap, brew berry tea

in token *Teacher* mug; eschew the news, let
Katherine Jenkins sing me 'Time to Say Goodbye'

while coal tits flit in hawthorn, heart-throb close.
Across the field a ruined house, sky-roofed, wall-fallen

damps my mood; removes me to a childhood kitchen
table, knots my chest, pools sudden desolation

– my brother, sister go away to school:
the first cocoon I knew about to come unwound.

Serendipity

Not the dizzy height of buildings,
the zippy grid of avenues and streets,
the traffic frenzy, multi-ethnic faces,
incessant walking feet; the energy, pizzazz,
Times Square world rendezvous; Macy's
retail labyrinth – enough to know it covers
seven blocks! Not all the pageantry
of Central Park or Broadway glitz:

to me this city's gift remains
a slender book: pre-used, green covered,
pocket-sized, picked up at a stall
on 57th Street – just as the taxi to the airport
came – such luck! *Gitangali, Song Offerings*
by Tagore: his sacred thirst. Sipping these
liquid lotus mysteries I'm quickened
with the pulse that is New York

In a Flash

for Noel Monahan

Two baby foxes – russet smears
streak out of April fields with cub-wild speed;
sense surface grit, light-dazzle, fur-frizzing sound,

keep going, blind –
I stiffen, clench the steering wheel,
unable to avert the fatal thump.

Sprung from a book launch, poetry-drunk,
we rhymers earth abruptly;
bemoan the blight of unintended hurt.

Connection

I hold your cherub body to my cheek
before the sideboard mirror, Eve
– my daughter's daughter –
in navy polka dots and scarlet bow.

You're nearly five months old
and want to look at everything.
Greedy for your smiles, I *kissy-kiss*
my lips to catch your eye.

Mesmerized by glint on crystal bowls,
framed photos silver gleam, you give
a quick, appeasing beam, then drop
your gaze to trawl the dazzling hoard.

When you leave I scribble lines
to keep the trade between us,
break its seal; defeat myself
with words that fail to sing.

Glimpsing the sacred image on the wall,
my anchor when I'm all awry –
think God a grandmother
delighting in our every move and whim.

First Things First

Her heyday in the forties
echoed older women's voices,
sounded marriage intimations like a gong:

Go before you're thirty –

William, intellectual, well read,
improvident in matters of finance;
heart bowed to head:

Go before you're thirty –

Barney, snazzy dancer, suave,
'Yours are the nicest hands I've ever held'
– indifference to confession, a disconcerting knell.

Go before you're thirty –

Wheels of fortune sped her on
to One – dependable, resolute, strong,
enterprising, handsome even, bold.

What harm largesse outdid imagination:
a double box of chocolates for her birthday –

Go before you're thirty?
Say but the word!

When All's Said and Done

It was 1944, Ascension Day ...
She never tired of telling how they met.
Inhaling deep, she'd launch into the tale:
A teacher, loosed from duty, off she set
to cycle to the hairdressers in town
– perhaps exchange a cardigan she'd bought;

spied a fellow on the margin of a crowd
gathered round a politician courting votes.
His companion reading signals sharply nudged:
If you've business to look after, now's your time.
He caught her on a hill as up she trudged;
a date for Sunday night was worth the climb.

Asked at ninety, lately widowed, how they met,
sighing lightly, she looked wistful, *I forget!*

Cyclamen

Chic as a Philip Treacy hat,
the cyclamen bloom I pluck
from its mouse-tail stem, struck
by its upswept sail-set look,
condones my theft.

I deftly flick it inside out,
unpack a simple flower form:
five pointed petals, flattened
smartly back; fluted calyx –
a fairy nectar cup.

Cyclamen by name and hue,
magnificent in winter dearth,
the subtle shift a twist can make,
my mother's invocation of panache:
It's all in the way you pitch your cap!

A Dream of my Father

He walked into the kitchen
of our childhood home: my father,
five years gone – collapsed at a cattle mart,
dispatched to hospital to no avail.

A sketchy web of relatives
goose-fleshed the room; electrified
by tacit pact, conspired to ignore his death,
cautioned not to register alarm.

In an overcoat too large,
no hat, he didn't speak.
I went to hug him, horror/pity torn;
sensed him recoil, his face distressed.

Preoccupied, he muttered something.
Left. I knew he went upstairs
to Mother's bedroom. We traded glances,
froze; implored she wouldn't be afraid.

This man who scaffolded my growing:
his strong, judicious influence more felt
than spoken, now holds ajar
a door I hadn't thought to open.

Goldfinches

A charm of goldfinches adorns
the peanut feeder hung from
the clothesline post. Scarlet faces,

black-bangled eyes intimidate
the regulars – some tits and other
finches. White-wimpled heads;

black, yellow-barred, white-dotted
wings; buff boleros; tail tips
snow-dipped set them apart.

These showy little creatures
stop my washing at the sink
and mulling over scraps

such entities don't grapple with –
settling their disparities
without the heaviness of thought

– small mysteries I'm daily gifted:
their unselfconscious gaiety
when I am most in need of grace.

Poetry Imperative

It flickers like a firefly
in a crevice of my brain:
lit by something seen or heard,
caught in flight from heart to head
– even out of nowhere I can trace.

I reach for paper, one side used,
and pencil its entirety – a latent
lyric seam I prize; transfer it
to the laptop, gauge its shape, then
take it to the kitchen, mind aflame.

I prop it on the counter: sauté, simmer,
season, grill; scribble words around
the fringe – fresh insights, zingy images;
finger dictionary lists: that dinner lands
itself on plates, more luck than skill.

When deadlines loom, it's headspin time
– no cobwebs chased, no hoover run.
Files closed, the muse plays mute. Life
rushes in; its flux and flow consumes
– till all at once its music draws me in.

Happenstance

He sat beside me as the Luas, sardine-packed,
whirred out from Connolly: broad-built, calm,
a cross between my father and any countryman
you'd meet at ease with women.

Day trippers, dripping wet, both come from
Longford – he in overcoat and cap, en route
to have his hearing aids assessed, I set to shuttle
on to visit family; we chatted of the benefit

the travel pass affords and parted at the stop.
Next morning at the checkout in a local store
a flash of recognition – face to face again;
each tickled at the trick of strangers being

twice in such proximity, we smiled and spoke
of chance, exchanged anonymous yet intimate
regard. As I recount the incident in print, he likely
winds the yarn in Derryharrow or Dromard.

Bona Fide

According to the legend – Colmcille,
voice choked with guilt, the hidden script a halter,
sought to defend his stealth with ink and quill,
the sacred text of Abbot Finnian's Psalter.
What blame for him, who under Finnian's skill,
caught fire of God as thirst for living water?
His ill-judged enterprise set will to will,
till Diarmaid deemed the copy: *Mother's daughter.*
Vindicated, Finnian raised his head,
illicit cull of Scripture overthrown.
Revenge of Colmcille left thousands dead;
at Cúl Dreimhne seeds of penitence were sown.
In exile, beyond books, his heart aflame,
to Iona, Colmcille bequeathed his name.

*

You'd have to sympathise with Colmcille,
especially when you eye your crowded shelves;
without enduring hours of cramp and chill,
we're swamped with books not scripted by ourselves.
I've done it in a small way, haven't you
– swiped lines you love from cherished books on loan?
assimilated thought that's somehow new,
not claimed its wisdom, beauty as your own.
It's tempting to dismiss these feuding monks,
bound to the Word without which none can thrive,
confined by limitations we can't count,
no more immune than we to envy, pride.
Today, proliferation is our bane, while
only words that smite the heart remain.

A Week Away

Where would you like to go? my travel-savvy
sister asks. I plump for Rome.

I'll be your guide, she tenders
– ever one to raise the stakes.

I keep her silhouette in view, her auburn hair
through narrow streets, broad sidewalks –

hijab, sari, cassock cloaked, the pair
of us footloose, her gusto jizzing up my sloth.

Majestic kerbside churches – a litany of saints:
John Lateran, Mary Major, Peter, Paul Outside

the Walls; the Pantheon – its roundness,
height, antiquity; its oculus an eye of Heaven.

San Clemente, church-on-church descent
to Mithraic temple room; unearthed

by a Longford son: Mullooly, Joseph,
Abbey Prior – his tomb a puff of pride.

Thunder splashed at Trevi Fountain, heat oppressed,
we sidle up and down the Spanish Steps.

Awed by dropouts on the pavement, silent, prone
– broken columns of the Forum strewn about

for contemplation, we diverge and come together
at the ghostly Coliseum, sun-glared St Peter's Square.

Dine on unctuous antipasti, side street, Trip Advisor
tipped; lick pistachio/mint gelato from our lips.

Stroll Trastevere's night-enchanted cobblestone,
Arrivederci Roma, in my heart I take you home.

In the Moment

i.m. Rita Cullen

The picture shows you ambling up the lane
in summer dress, chic for a 1940s ordinary day,
your arms enclosing crumpled clothes, the whiff
of roses, fresh-aired cotton, meadowsweet.

Your hair a sweep of waves falls over your left eye;
your gaze interrogates the camera bearer:
perhaps a visitor arrived too soon ... like death
not far ahead that snuffed your voice

in the back of a homebound hackney car, after the fall
– the doctor couldn't hold you – the trap upended
when the pony shied, startled by headlights at a cross,
your children jolted, thrown ...

But, in this moment, as you near the house,
its thatch and whitewashed walls, I come to you –
the aunt, whose tragic fate, screen played
my early narrative, whose face I never knew.

Here, in the shelter of tall trees your father planted,
I hold with you the riches of your life –
a vision of the flint and flower of being;
leave to the road ahead its shade and light.

FULL BLOWN

A single yellow rose, autumnal, pale,
slender glass vase posed,
fragranced the hall for days.

How did I not expect its later state?
– a cluster of silken petals
hushed on the polished table.

Its purpose filled, the stem remained
persuasive in a different mode:
a paean of surrender.

The House in the Wood

i.m. Kathleen and John McKenna

The sign has changed from *Sale Agreed* to *Sold,*
reverberations ripple through the trees;
the erstwhile owners lent enchantment here,
the winding pebble path their memory holds.

The grownup children of the neighbourhood
remember tapping on the door; dream
Kathleen's smile, inviting; step inside, spill
stored-up fantasies, confessions, boasts; ruffle

the grass-green shaggy rug; float questions
never aired at home; hear tales of valour,
fairy lore: discussion prompts; opinions
handled gently as the Hummels overhead.

Before they notice, Johnny slips away; returns
with orange in a jug, eye-popping ever ready
treats. Tumblers emptied, crumbs dispersed,
like proper visitors they sense it's time to go.

With mock regret, their hosts propel them home,
sink back into seclusion; their wealth
to know child innocence the antidote of age –
their legacy unseen as seeds in undergrowth.

Sequence

Snowdrops prop us up
when winter tries to topple us.

Crocus cups in clusters –
purple, saffron light the shade.

Daffodil profusion sparks
a yellow surge of confidence.

In gardens, windowboxes,
tulips elegant and spare.

Pungent flowering currant
shakes out pocketfuls of memory.

Forsythia's flamboyance –
flagrant, zingy yellow blaze.

Snowy blackthorn prickles hedges,
melts to hawthorn's cream extravagance.

Plum petals, cherry blossom
render pathways nuptial trails.

Buds fatten, imperceptibly explode,
till every leaf on every tree unfolds.

Birds' urgent tunes stir purpose,
root out old excuses;

Find within our wilted yearnings,
tender shoots.

Refuge

She's led into the section where we sit,
my passenger and I, now hours in A&E.
Her weathered skin, dishevelled hair,
unsteady gait, her fragile frame
– no older than my daughter – jolt me.

Alone, she gazes straight ahead,
lips gripped, chin raised: an island
in a hectic sea; a boat inured
to turbulence, here moored
by distant faces, fractured limbs.

The man who pours the tea delivers us:
his humming cheerfulness a gift we sip,
lifting the air. She'll have to take it
day by day she whispers, her gentleness
a dignity no circumstance can veil.

Past midnight, word relays: they'll keep
my friend for observation. As I leave,
this woman wishes me safe home.
I want to take her hand, but don't,
sensing a deeper bond already forged.

Her courage, not her torment, escorts me
to my car. The concourse bare, an ambulance
pulls out in front, a godsend at this hour,
a beacon on a lonely road – we need not
wade the whole morass alone.

Take Heart

after Elizabeth Bishop's 'One Art'

You get quite used to loss – in fact things slide
so stealthily you hardly notice their departure:
sturdiness, long vistas, drive.

Don't grieve your fading looks: slack neck,
receding gums – it's a continuum. The caterpillar
turns to mush, emerges winged! You'll soon

be dropping claim to all you own without regret.
My childhood home is gone – confinement too –
a shop, a little river. A scenic village hosts me now;

my early ripples feed a greater river. I've lost
my youth and yours, our strengths and limits pooled.
We'll die, of course, but death is not disaster.

The bursting bud, unerring sunrise, kindness
all attest to life: life limitless – the joy we glimpse,
the love we miss. Listen! Birds whistle it
– there must be life hereafter.

Even to Think Kindly

When dents within collide
and discord stings the air; when
humours won't align, we each
move out, inhabit different spheres.

Apart, our spirits yield and twists
unwind. As if the other senses it,
a tenderness returns. With evening
comes conclusion, and night

smooths harrowed grooves.
I sing the overlap of things –
the inward pull, the outward flow,
close cycles in love's school.

Just This

It came to me
on angel breath.

I wrote it down
to hold it –

just this:
to be utterly me
here
in this moment.

Late wisdom adds:
whatever facet
of the self that be;

beyond condition, form,
to essence –

more aspirational
than set;

more prompt
than programme.

Everyday Wonder

Luke rises, wobbles on his not yet
twelve-month feet, across the deeply
pattered floor – how fortunate I'm here
for this. Distracted by things coming into

reach, being just as quickly snatched
– his brother's blaring bugle, his sister's
dangling tracksuit string – he totters on,
arms raised like wings for balance.

Heart-stoppingly, he almost runs; from
knee to knee, he takes off shrieking;
steadies, staggers, plops; clambers to
his feet again, makes for his mother's lap

and chuckling, nuzzles in. Feeling the tug,
she cuddles him, resettles him on track.
Kissing his curls, his father turns him,
steers him past the point of no return.

Parenthood

We become superfluous
to our children in a way they
never grow superfluous to us:

our hearts enshrine them,
exulting in their least success,
repining when they fall or fail.

What wisdom dreamed up
such a scheme for love.

Woodland on my Doorstep

The steep descent from road access,
darkened by overhanging trees,
taps hidden childhood depths;
scatters the day's dilemmas.

The space within me widens
to absorb the whiff of wildness.
I tramp the undulating trails, round
bends that mimic life's vicissitudes;

stand still; absorb the silence,
riffed by distant wheeze of mallards
on Lough Ree, sporadic barks –
excitement or defence on nearby paths.

A plane above the heaped-up cloud
drones other worlds. Now, muffled
rhythmic twitter, deep in matted bramble,
softens my footsteps crunch.

Well-intentioned caution fails to curb
my walking in the woods alone
when house bounds can't contain me;
vague fears of misadventure fade

before the graciousness of trees,
Rapunzel-clinging ivy braids,
alluring grooves and crevices,
of lake-lapped stone.

Fresh shoots from stunted roots,
propped broken limbs, unhurried
constant change – consistent
promise notes my spirit sings.

Kilbeggan Gifts

Identity of place – a midland crib
my father happened on by chance;

a sibling base, repository of memories
prismatic in their reach;

the shop he kept to keep us: its counter,
store and yard the contours of our youth;

mix of town and country folk, some
faces I can conjure still;

nature, lyric, mother influence,
religion, erudition to the fore;

the Convent School, nuns' habits, rules:
wheat and darnel of our growing years;

the Hill, its little houses leaning on each other;
trudging up on bikes, exhilarating down;

the Square, its set-back buildings, fanlight doors;
pump-handle cranks, dusk chasing games;

the Church, high-end of town, side gallery
for Sunday Mass, the choir for posing;

the Races, not the glamour nor the risk –
sawdust, shilling jingle, hawker blitz;

water churning whitely, Locke's Distillery
big wheel; weighbridge waver, whiskey whiff;

cemented Brosna stretch; swim lessons,
pride afloat, deflated swell at summer's close.

Sweetheart strolls on riverbank; 'Red Sails
in Sunset' waltz, first flushes of romance.

The only tie now parents' graves; community
remembrance rite, last Sunday of July.

GENESIS OF PASSION

She wouldn't miss the Knit & Stitch Show
at the RDS, her yearly fillip: fabrics,
dreamcatchers, tea cosies, scarves,
hats to sell at charity bazaars.

Where did it start – this joy creation,
fireside art? A spark a neighbour in her
childhood lit, lured her to sew and knit;
a sack, a lucky dip to rummage in –

buttons, sequins, zigzag braid to pick.
At eight, a rag doll's pinafore she made
rivalled her mother's cut-down suits.
She remembers she was hooked.

Her grandchildren declare her table
a disaster zone; swipe strips of satin,
velvet, crepe, create impromptu marvels,
stride a Silk Road of their own.

Recipe for Ease

to sit in the brown recliner chair
of soft faux leather; fit my
flex points to its contours;
pick something rich to read
from the rising pile of soul food
on the low, side table ...

close my eyes; tune in to sounds:
wind gusting up the garden, car tyres
creasing the wet road, the subtle
shift and rustle of your paper
as you solve the day's Sudoku;
hum of the fridge, tick of the clock;

retrace my steps since daybreak; list
conscious gifts; locate beloved faces ...
drift ... Next I know I'm back,
all fibres stretched,
re-patterned in the tapestry
– complexity eroded bit by bit.

La Sieste

for Tom

I've grown attached to Van Gogh's couple
sleeping in a cornfield, ochre, blue. In them
I recognise our sleeping selves: your
barefoot, flat-backed sprawl, hands lapped
behind your head, hat drawn across your eyes
the way you drop the paper on your face,

catnapping in the chair at home. And me:
the compliant lie of me, my folded arms
a bolster for your ribs, my elbow snug
in your armpit. Swathed in speedwell blue
to match your shirt, my slumber-leaden thighs
support your loin; our newly-flowered love.

We're in our early wedded days: for you
enough to have me there – at ease with my
intricate heart. You've planned our rest
in welcome shade; freed the animals to feed;
settled straw to bed us, sickles safely laid:
provident as Boaz to my complicit Ruth.

I'd like Van Gogh to know how well he
captured us: still folded in conflicting modes
not inconsistent with content. I've found myself
in blossom-scattered fields; you lose yourself
in images you screen and hone. On level ground,
we daily weigh the steady harvest of enduring care.

Promise

Dreamy bramble buds
about to burst their downy orbs,
streak ice cream pink at seams,
as streamers on a wedding car
leak colours of the gowns.

Trace back to spring's first thrust:
bud clusters in a pouch of leaves
uncurl and climb, blossom in turn,
pinhead-stamen flushed; gift
winged and creeping things.

On sunny banks where flowers thrive
– May, mild and mostly dry –
bees' nectar feast yields honey glut,
and blackberries abound
in hedge and field.

A Time for Everything

I watch you from the kitchen window
fasten twine to guide the drill you dig;

slide a lath along to smooth the ridge;
poke finger holes, arm's length apart –

dark funnels for the seed you scatter
from a packet in your pocket; sift clay

for finer cover; fist fertilizer pellets from
the yellow bowl I used to use for baking.

Through the wishbone of your thighs,
your back arched over, supple still,

I sense your core alignment amid
daffodils, warm sunshine, robin twitter.

As if I knew. Did even you suppose
this yearly planting ritual had run its course?

A Moment Seized

Mark 2: 1–12

Such crowded days, he has to leave his bed
to pray. Back in Capernaum the fever
spreads: they crush to glimpse his face.

And when a crippled stretchered one
can't even reach the door, his bearers
strip the roof; rope him steady to the floor.

Whoa! People shift and shuffle back; shook
plaster-dust drops down like powdered
rain, and Jesus laughs and fluffs his hair;

his touch relieves the astronaut's unease.
Be healed in heart! Your brothers too
are rescued by their faith. A step too far

for Pharisees – *How dare he make such claims!*
Indulgently he enters their alarm: *Which is*
easier to say – Be cleansed of sin, or Walk?

Silence rings like tinnitus; excitement peaks.
He speaks the word: the cripple limbers,
stands. The key to sift the riddle is at hand.

Orchid Watching

A poem is growing in our kitchen: this
orchid by the windowsill my sister's gift:

its spindled inflorescence,
regardless of the seasons, a ballerina's lift.

Inspiring poise, its timing stills.
Each blossom opened, waxy, plump

and barely pink, endures for weeks;
secures the ripening of a bud

along the stem. The bud balloons,
splits crimson-seamed, a complex

symmetry: a freckled, iridescent face.
And soon a pink flotilla thrills –

life now a carousel and death a myth;
but one by one, dry tissues drop,

and stems, arched gracefully, zigzag
where pleasures hung. Furred roots

curve up for air; broad fleshy leaves
like matching sails, keep hope afloat.

St Brigid's Way

A group text on St Brigid's Eve
instructed me to leave
a piece of cloth out overnight
to catch St Brigid's blessing.

Sceptical, yet game, I chose a sea green
silken scarf with threads of gold –
a present from Morocco – sealed in plastic
against snail trails, insect traffic, damp.

Next morning, walking early through
the house, I noticed trucks out front;
heard clatters, thuds, loud shouts –
men getting set to work.

The path, I breathed, *the long awaited*
footpath into town. Elation bubbled:
I recalled the date, my doorstep scarf ...
declared I'd name the path *St Brigid's Way.*

Mid breakfast, rising whines outside
stirred doubt a furtive glance confirmed:
no gang in sight, an angry blade
laid waste a scrubwood site.

I quickly put my silly scarf away, glad
no one knew how far my wits had strayed:
this mind that gallops wildly on a hunch, trails
Brigid's peerless ploy to raise a church.

TRAIN MUSINGS

Pity grips me as I glimpse through
sky-wide windows, scatters of cattle
grazing or staring at the fleeting train.

Mild and aloof, it's not their nature
to leave hoof marks on a human frame.
Such freak reports: a woman

trampled in a gateway, a man
knocked senseless in his field,
reveal these creatures, void of malice,

prey to consternation; and though
they suffer for our sustenance, at
carbon cost, consumption mounts –

a quandary for our world. A shudder
calls to mind a day, when you, a child,
came home from rambling in the fields;

showed us how you lay back
on the grass as cattle circled round,
loving their stillness, breath ...

Lulled by the motion, jovial hum,
I close my eyes, return you to
the freedom of your childhood bounds.

Tweet Tweet

for Jimmy

A text alerts – he's trimming gooseberries
for jam; enquires what I'm at. I know at once
it's not a test, much less an intimate suggestion;
rather a whim to fling the social net.

I say: I'm sharing strawberries with my spouse;
appreciate his quest. See him smile, await
replies from others on his list, while I resume
my own discursive trip. We can no more

corral our thoughts than we can cage the air:
flash memories, rehashed conversations,
random rifts, a disparate array of persons,
dear and distant, backdrop humdrum chores

while mindfulness pleads focus. Now smart
phones can outsmart themselves by hours,
constant chatter build a cyber Babel Tower,
I still glisten at the whistle of a text.

Stirrings

A letter from my brother on the mat
delights me – an out of season gift.
Just retired and ripe for flourishing,
he's at the West Cork Literary Festival,
in sunshine more accustomed in Corfu
or Cannes: not that he claims to write,
unless the force of characters our hometown
harboured drives him to pen them down.

An only brother between pairs of sisters,
he's his own man: modest, unobtrusive,
passionate. Beguiled by stories of old
rogues our father spun, time and again,
the phone alight, he'll yarn the night away.
Maybe this letter challenge, set to let
the writing flow, will open a new channel
of expression, of transport yet unknown.

The Way we Were

Country people brought their flowers to town,
first fruits to boost the annual display of faith:
lupins, rocket, peonies bloomed in buckets;
scented my father's General Merchant store.

At nightfall, children watched as men
in braces, sleeves rolled up, swung picks,
bored holes with crowbars, verged the road.
By morning, trees had grown on either side

– our street become the Champs Elysee.
Now every house a hive of busyness: swept
doorsteps decked with posies; starched table
cloths posed Blessed Martins, Sacred Hearts.

At two o'clock, all pathways led to church.
An order formed: Canopy Bearers, Children
of Mary, Men's Sodality, Kilbeggan School
Boys' Band, Non-Classifieds and Also-Rans.

My brother on tin whistle, smirked in kilt
and feathered cap; small boys in short pant
suits, girls veiled in white first off the mark,
blew flower kisses in the Saviour's path.

The Rosary was broadcast, hymns were sung;
stray thoughts and dreamy words wove incense
mingled clouds. We sauntered down The Hill,
like extras in a film, fell in and out of step;

turned serpentine at Mary's Statue, sloped
back up – the Green our goal. Traffic halt:
a moment of importance. Men knelt on caps,
heads bowed; new headscarves added flair.

Children poked tar bubbles; played *I spy*.
The choir struck up *Tantum Ergo;* bells tinkled
summer air. My child heart drew communion,
secure in a world that knew the rules.

Final Call
in memory of Sean Cahill (1931–2015)

The stately ash has fallen, its roots ripped up
in a winter gale that whipped the lake at Ballyclare.

Driving past, I grieve for him who hailed
its seasonal demeanour year on year; who

one May morning after, alert to secret summoning,
intrepidly set sail for the further shore.

The tree lies fractured in the quiet field that merges
with Lough Ree. Stark branches forking skyward

open leaves, host perching birds, as if not everything
has changed. We gather numbly, murmur praise,

as if by words we'd reignite the spark of him
who kindled warmth within, set hearts at ease.

In silent labyrinths his spirit lingers; his words,
his wisdom sing on still connected strings.

Nursing Home Visit

A bit like school, we sit and face
each other in the big, bright, airy room:
a pick-me-up of poetry buffs aspire
to lift the spirits of the long confined.

Feeble, drowsy, strained, they try to catch
the drift of airs and rhymes, as Mary plays
Oh Danny Boy, Believe Me. Carers, intimate
and kind, kindle the spark of each – a wink,

a touch, a smile roll back the years –
these people in their prime: self-guided,
moving mountains, holding forts
– threads lost in a fog of time.

Bearers of the tune, they count on us
to flourish in their name. When Paddy plays
the national anthem, wheelchairs hamper,
passions rise; we chant our common heritage.

One man, eyes closed, mouths every word
– transported to the Hogan Stand:
the ball thrown in, a mounting score –
Roscommon coast to glory in Croke Park.

Evening on the 25A

An Indian girl of dark and shining beauty sits
beside me, quickly bobs in sleep; in front

a flax-blonde woman, eight studs in either ear,
jokes with her friend, at home in mother tongue.

A heavily-fleshed man discomfited with
narrow seats, talks loudly on his phone;

at the Chapelizod stop, a golden Labrador
emerges from behind his feet, follows

as he hits the road, bearing his weight
as lightly as he can. A fresh contingent

blusters in; young gallants stand, surrender
needed rests. Outside, construction crews –

hard hats and yellow vests – drive metal poles
into the future. Phones signal texts;

work-weary fingers scroll fluorescent screens.
A city visitor returning west, I flit

between estrangement and belonging,
each measuring the mystery we fit.

WINTER MELODY

for Jack Harte

Crows, crotchet black, sketch
grace notes on cloud-stencilled ash;

perch long enough to scan
the food potential, rest;

directed by a hidden cue,
undo the score, fly off to roost;

etch primal silhouettes
across a pearl-grey sky:

their wake, a wordless void,
a dirge for the departing birds.

The Nuns are Leaving Lanesboro

They would have made inspiring wives,
accommodating grandmothers, these brides
of Christ. They could be architects, explorers,
had God not other patterns for their lives.

Dispatched from Ballymahon Convent,
three shrewd young sisters forged a pathway
to the Shannon brink; swapped lofty arches,
leafy walks for homely psalms, a roadside hearth.

In time, they put down roots, established schools,
a convent; furthered education for our girls.
Through sixty years we gave our children to them,
drew sustenance ourselves from deeper pools.

New freedoms came: return to girlhood names,
old habits laid aside. We all became more human:
single, married, cloistered found a crucial link,
each mirroring love's nucleus to each.

We'll miss their hospitality, its chapel sanctuary,
their joy in our prosperity, their blessing in distress.
The mustard seed has flourished, flowered,
seeded; and yet, their going makes us weep.

Approaching a Poem

To rhyme or not to rhyme
sidesteps the question –

how does the poem stir you,
draw you in;

what rhythm does it strike,
which vowels chime;

where does the poem take you –
familiar quarters, thresholds new;

how does its argument
intrigue, repel, delight you,

punch words imprint your mind,
spur you to track its import line by line;

what notion of your conscious self
emerges; what alien view

prompts you to find within yourself
the poem that is you?

Finding Feet

A board he salvaged from an old
abandoned house became his base,

smashed mirror scoffing at ill-luck:
young artists can't afford such stuff.

Strife-ripped, he severed posters: head
blitz, wing clip, confusion's eye – a child!

How would he cope with fatherhood,
his girl with monumental change –

their bright unfettered love weighed down?
The child arrives: a boy – amazement, joy

beyond their dreams. Distress of early days
gives way to calm: the little fellow taps

inherent trust, takes milestones in his stride:
first smile, first tooth, first shoes.

Child vision rules; new quandaries wrest
new questions – a constant Rubik's cube.

Green paint in stream, aspiring lines,
fluidity, his toddler's trailing lace.

SIGNIFICANCE

When a poem comes together
there's a private kind of joy

like the neverending pleasure
in a child you've helped to form;

the distressing situation you
discover you can bear;

the carefully sourced outfit
you know you'll smile to wear;

the random pot appearance
of a flower you haven't sown,

the surfeited fulfilment of
preserving fruit you've grown;

the primal satisfaction
when you deftly mend a rent;

the startling green of hawthorn,
April ushers by a fence;

the thrill a fox can shiver,
crossing paths with you alone;

the daily invitations,
overarching wisdom borne.

Can a Flower Speak to Loss?

Some babies – like the kadupul flower –
live only a few hours, maybe less;

breathe all their essence, warmth, fulfilment
and are gone on angel breath;

leave their imprint, fragrance named,
a long indelible caress.

The kadupul takes a year to peak,
exults in star-white bloom one single night;

by dawn it droops, and like a tiny human form
– however delicate – forever marks its sphere.

An orchid – water lily, cactus-type,
it grows in forks of trees; dangles

long, scalloped buds from slender stems:
bright wonder, destined not to linger here.

Enchanted by its mystery, allure,
Mexico to Venezuela; Sri Lanka

to Japan, they name it for fragility:
Midnight Miracle, Queen of the Night,

Flower from the Heavens – so brief
an advent of unbounded life.

Mother Rule

I couldn't help but focus
on the frail, determined lady
escorted up the aisle by two
distinctly stylish daughters.

Their anxious, sidelong glances
at the tremble of her leaflet,
the strain to lift her foot across
the kneeler don't distract her.

In a sunbeam's stained-glass light,
I see a keen-eyed mother, seating
two small girls in tartan skirts, their
dangling feet discreetly kept in line.

Spine-warped, hair winter white, she
dignifies infirmity. Authority a plum
and ochre scarf about her neck nudges
her elder daughter at communion time.

October 2017
for Michael

A kind of rust has struck the trees;
the beeches lit with sunlight make
a carnival of roads and fields.

We all have our time to shine,
and yours is fading fast, dear brother
– unless surrender is our finest state.

Childhood playmates, we were a match
before life placed a stretch between us,
not bridged enough, now painfully

past reach. Pilfered of speech – your
scintillation, relish of food and drink,
your courage strikes us mute.

And you, with stock integrity, serenely
bear this crucial nerve erosion; defy
its limitation. So lately fired by travel,

discourse, humour, music, sport
– though the carnival is over, your trust
in trees' new greening is our hope.

Dreaming of my Mother

Again I dreamt my mother out of reach,
a place I didn't recognise, myself
distressed: How could I not be conscious
of her whereabouts at ninety-plus?

I could see her standing somewhere vague
– her very forthright self, in crimplene dress,
glasses on nose, like someone silenced
in a gameshow, a prompter just offstage.

I wrestled guilt, confusion; quizzed my
sister as to what she knew, and how,
unknown to me, she managed to maintain
connection, while puzzling how

all this could be – my mother's death
some years back an occluded fact.
The dream dissolves in frantic resolution
to get my daughter-duty back on track.

Relief to wake and know the trial is over:
my mother safely where her heart's at rest;
our parent-caring rotas done, her
nursing home confinement spent.

She wouldn't want my least disturbance;
though prone herself to angst, in later
years her overriding attitude was gladness –
delight in little jaunts beneath the sky.

Coming of Age in the Poetry Circle

Late autumn sun emblazes fading leaves,
red apples linger lightly on old trees; here
framed in public view by shelves of books,
we elders forge year round enduring trust.

The circle widens, gains another chair; poems
leap from well-thumbed books, one issues from
a screen, another comes heart-honed; skilled
saxaphonist's silver tone cues keyboard rhapsody.

Life pulses here; book borrowers are struck;
the lilt, the glint, the lift – time shrunk to this:
war, climate chaos, inequality aside,
immersion in what fills us is our gift.

To the Core

The kitchen can be any style, the dramas vary;
not only children being raised, but parents:
intrinsic skills found passed through generations.

How else could they withstand the death of self,
occlusion of each other? Only to find their children
thrive, fabric of new life a patchwork wonder.

One child stretches limits, impatient to achieve;
another animates his toys, adapts to any change;
the last-born slips through gaps the others leave.

Now, this winsome three-year-old, off-form,
harangues about some food – the way he wants or
doesn't want it. His mother meshed in myriad

concerns, runs patience thin. Her plucky prized
appendage from his birth, unused to caution, weeps;
they melt into each other. So integral the alchemy

of family ferment, they barely notice bubbles rise.
For me, at this remove, eyes mist their raw
abandon: child to mother, mother to her child.

Last Dance

'Your mother never saw us dance',
his lame defence against
her rumbling discontent.

From 'Kerry Set' they
step-by-step advanced
to near concordance.

For her, romance concealed
recurring gaps; for him,
she had become the dance.

His bid to sidestep pain,
lanced all their fragile plans.
Her mother never saw them dance.

CORNUCOPIA

Your husbandry this season yielded
copious cobs of corn, wrenched one by one
from slender stalks I watched grow tall
as high-heeled girls, swish leafy skirts,
all summer framed by the kitchen window.

So fat and snug they feel, tight-wrapped
in layers of leaves – a *pass the parcel,*
children's party treat. Each peel reveals
ribbed tissue – paler, finer every tier.
The music stops, the children squeal:

smooth seams of butter-yellow beads,
glossy, plump, exact as buttons on
an abacus appear. And I am back, a callow
lass, one summer in New York; agog
at such diversity – colour, brashness, accent,

marital fluidity, city rush and heat;
boardwalk ambles, rollerbladers, sunburn
beach – my guardians keen to give me safe
experience: cherries from street vendors,
hotdogs, coleslaw, cobs of corn.

Now images converge in your dig-happy
streak – this homegrown veg exotic,
garden bounty amid cauliflower, sprouts
and strawberries, perennial abundance:
your labour love a finger-licking feast.

Indomitable Wings
i.m. Sophie Mary Pierce 1896–1939

Powerlessness must breed defiance
unless the spirit dies. Imagine infant
Sophie Pierce, found sitting by her
mother's corpse, ash of her father's ire;
how would this child survive?

Desperate to redress the crime,
her father's sisters claimed her; set
boundaries schoolgirl Sophie spurned:
lithe-limbed, strong-willed,
she leaped and ran unrivalled.

London in her twenties, science bent,
drove rescue expeditions, sport events:
tennis, cycles, javelin hurls; cut women's
style to suit, men driven wild – marriage
a concession to furnish her desires.

Fired by athletic feats, Olympic coup, now,
'Mary, Lady Heath', she dared the skies:
defying patriarchy, learned to fly; crash
landed on a football match; flew solo from
South Africa in leopard skin and pearls.

A blinding drive to conquer:
issue of blood or strife, the sky her
fairground, peril pitch, this Irish
'Lady Icarus', despite a manic Daedalus,
grace winged her star-crossed life.

CROSSINGS

We do not choose the bridges
we must cross, they just appear
before us, break our stride: imprisoned,
shamed, deserted, dispossessed;
hit with unremitting illness,
stricken by the suffering of a child.

No point in looking back,
imagining alternate paths;
there's only this bridge, however
stark, or rickety its span. You press
the planks beneath your feet, grip
the handrail, knuckle-bleached;

you whimper, howl and rally, try
to float and sink or hide, till you
wake and face your terror; meet
an angel by a river, find a place
of calm inside, and the bridge
become a runway – you can fly.

BEYOND BELIEF

i.m. Carmel and Jimmy Casey (2018)

It's not as if we didn't know their virtue:
each sheltering, a haven as a pair; nor
that they hadn't drained the dregs of sorrow –
their Carrowstrawley home, a cup of cheer.

That illness should waylay them both together;
pluck them abruptly from the homing tide:
such obstacles they met with equanimity; long
beach walks, hand-in-hand, dream kept alive.

Having endured the ravages of treatment,
at one with whom she trusted as her life,
unflinching, Carmel felt the veil grow thinner;
slipped, garlanded in peace, through Easter light.

And Jimmy, plundered, frail, undone without her,
left everything not stored in each dear face;
then aptly on the eve of Pentecost,
the Spirit bound their souls in stellar space.

Solace

My spirit favours quiet places,
shady byways, nooks
– not that I'm shy of company,
find all my sustenance in books.

Your tightening arms around me,
nights when longings coincide;
ways we soften towards
each other after hurts.

Daily faces on the street,
the supermarket aisle, the joy of
commonality, the neverending
food providers' choir.

And babies: petal fragile thereness;
all-mouth-and-fist survival, sated
eye roll, angel smiles, unconscious
benediction, each an unrepeated chime.

That spiders spin intricate webs
unseen, and hoarfrost silvers
stems and leaves, an artist's filigree
– exigencies of prayer.

Oh, and river music: I could settle
on a bed of moss, the sky my dome,
soothed by rhythm, suck and slosh
of water circumventing stone.

Alone on certain nights at home:
space all-encompassing;
love-hallowed rooms
aglow with presence.

Stealing a March

Corralled, removed from social
intercourse, at first unnerved
at being deemed unsafe, we soon
embrace a semi-cloistered state.

Close contact snaps in this huge health
hiatus; time empties of engagements;
sharp questions rise: what practices
to scrap, what gains to keep.

In tune with this unflush, risk-ridden
stretch, away from public scrutiny,
I flirt with a recurring wish –
to liberate my hair.

I view my head in different lights,
from every angle, mirrors poised –
the verdict undeniable: sunbleach
aside, a whiter shade of pale.

Each week, from wash to wash,
a frisson stirs: I part a dappled veil,
observe my lifelined face, in girlhood
spurred by adolescent curves.

I'm testing vivid colours kind
to white; bright, striking neckwear,
earring chic: 'Vanity of vanities' – yet
neither must we sail a sinking ship!

Covid Christmas

Longing spans the world
for dear ones stranded. Contagion
rages, cancels travel plans.
This Christmas has its own intent:
strict rhythms make us stoical,
designer masks now tokens of regard;
door welcome-wreaths contain a hint
of caution; stringed symphonies
of starry light, new galaxies come down.
A card depicts Nativity in tender mode,
essentials of the story told anew –
the deepest truth that holds us, tilted
between need for hugs, imperative
to keep apart for greater good.

Fandango

Joy: two long-bound lovers
playing hide-and-seek; he peering
round the doorpost as he leaves
to gauge the weather, she bobbing by
the window ledge to humour him;
– a remnant Christmas trinket by the sink:
two courting robins as the year begins –
a pledge, however they diverge
in colour palettes, pace,
their default stance, support,
assuagement for each other;
this recent frolic, eye-to-eye approach,
a deep nest, redbreast ember,
feathering to flame.

DANCING THE VILLANELLE

Approaching it like mastering a dance,
I set myself to learn the villanelle:
at three score years and ten, who can't advance?

Coming on the formula by chance,
I finally attempt to prise its shell:
approaching it like mastering a dance,

where formerly I always looked askance.
Well, at a céilí, under someone's spell –
at three score years and ten, who can't advance –

it's sometimes quite acceptable to prance:
The Waves of Tory rising to a swell;
approaching it like mastering a dance,

such capers often furthering romance –
though one be plump, another a gazelle;
at three score years and ten, who can't advance?

More energetic than gavottes in France,
my wits, in figuring this villanelle;
approaching it like mastering a dance,
at three score years and ten, who can't advance?

From Here to Where You Are

for Carmel

A tiny plaque you said you loved – who gave
to whom? – a toddler in a furry coat and curls,
set resolutely on a woodland path, uphill
ahead, arrests me. The caption reads –
'The journey to a friend's house isn't long'.
And on one birthday you expressed regret
your headstart meant your leaving me behind.
How could we have guessed how true
that sentiment would turn: how swiftly
you'd be swept to journey's end, and I bereft?
You knew the bends I round, the daily fuss;
led on by your assuring voice, your smile,
where hope dissolves and sorrows mend:
the essence of our friendship's thrust.

TREASURE HUNT

Convergence of a thank you card, some
Van Gogh bookmarks dropped in my lap,

reflections of a recent college graduate
– a busy junior infant once – now maps for me

an impetus then pulsing in my blood:
the years I slipped my shackles,

igniting fledgling intellects and souls
– endeavours we together owned: stories,

mischief, wisps of history, contingency,
creation, song; forays beyond the walls.

I carry poems within me now, like children
nudged in this or that direction for their good.

Occasional encounters with young adults
brave enough to speak of influence,

transport me back to often hectic days,
when morning always turned a pristine page;

and I, in all the energy of classroom buzz,
would sometimes have to pinch myself

to bear the privilege, contain excitement;
curb, too open a display of utter love.

About the Author

Margaret Nohilly, a native of Kilbeggan, County Westmeath, living in Lanesboro, County Longford for most of her life, is a retired primary teacher. She has been immersed in poetry for more than 25 years – the seed of which she traces to her mother's transport in voicing the poetry of her brother, Michael Walsh of Fore, County Westmeath. Margaret's own impetus to write began with Lasraí Writers, Lanesboro in 1995, and continues through the Poetry and Music Circle, a fortnightly gathering of poetry enthusiasts in Lanesboro Library. She is an avid participant in literary activities throughout County Longford. Her work is widely published. A chapbook of her early poems, *April Promise,* was published by Lapwing, Belfast in 2009.